write an
irresistible CV

Julie Gray

D1434459

flash.

Hodder Education
338 Euston Road, London NW1 3BH.

Hodder Education is an Hachette UK company

First published in UK 2011 by Hodder Education.

This edition published 2011.

British Library Cataloguing in Publication Data: a catalogue record for this title is available from the British Library.

10 9 8 7 6 5 4 3 2 1

The publisher has used its best endeavours to ensure that any website addresses referred to in this book are correct and active at the time of going to press. However, the publisher and the author have no responsibility for the websites and can make no guarantee that a site will remain live or that the content will remain relevant, decent or appropriate.

The publisher has made every effort to mark as such all words which it believes to be trademarks. The publisher should also like to make it clear that the presence of a word in the book, whether marked or unmarked, in no way affects its legal status as a trademark.

Every reasonable effort has been made by the publisher to trace the copyright holders of material in this book. Any errors or omissions should be notified in writing to the publisher, who will endeavour to rectify the situation for any reprints and future editions.

Hachette UK's policy is to use papers that are natural, renewable and recyclable products and made from wood grown in sustainable forests. The logging and manufacturing processes are expected to conform to the environmental regulations of the country of origin.

www.hoddereducation.co.uk

Typeset by MPS Limited, a Macmillan Company.
Printed in Great Britain by CPI Cox & Wyman, Reading.

Contents

Introduction

If you've got one minute to read this, you're spending longer than many recruiters will spend reading your CV. That doesn't mean it's not worth learning to write one — in fact the opposite is true. Teaching yourself to write an effective CV, instead of sending a poor quality one or paying someone else to write it, has enormous benefits beyond increasing your chances of getting an interview. The writing process itself can help to improve your understanding of employers' needs, awareness of your own skills, communication style, presentation and confidence.

Words matter

The words you use say a lot about you: they can give insight into your attitudes, beliefs and strengths, hopes, fears and weaknesses. They can also cause misunderstandings. A CV must be clear: convincing yet impressive, concise yet alluring, and true to who you are. The key is to be positive, while always thinking about things from a recruiter's perspective.

Build a factsheet

Your starting point is building your factsheet. This contains all the information you might need including personal details, qualifications and employment dates. Understanding what employers need and want to know is essential, as well as knowing which things you can (or indeed should) leave out.

Look at your skills

Spend time analyzing your own skills. Identify which skills you have and think up concrete examples of when you've put these skills to good use and what the result was. Examples can come from paid or unpaid work, interests or personal life. Useful techniques like SHORTlisting (see Chapter 3) can help you to distil these into short, punchy bullet points.

Create a generic CV

Set the tone for your CV with a brief summary or profile, based on the skills you've identified. Add your objectives and that's your draft 'generic' CV – the foundation for all that follows. Your time and effort is then best spent honing your language and adding power.

Refine, refine, refine

* Your words ... to suggest a person of action, with purpose, who delivers benefits.
* Your sentences ... to keep them short, meaningful and relevant.
* Your section order ... to keep 'what you offer an employer' firmly in the spotlight.

Always remind the reader why they should be interviewing *you*.

Target

The final edit is your most important: targeting or tailoring your CV. Show an employer you don't want just any job, but this one in particular, working for them. Do your research, and explain clearly why the fit between you, this role and this employer is so perfect. Target covering letters and application forms the same way.

Layout and presentation

Once the writing is finished, this takes over; it must be as strong as your CV content. Select the layout and format that feels right. Always do a quality check before sending. Write a covering letter that ensures your CV gets read.

That's it. Time to get started. Teach yourself a valuable new skill: how to write a great CV.

1

getting the basic details together

If you aren't sure whether your CV contains everything it should and nothing it shouldn't, or you've never written a CV before, this is the right starting point.

This chapter focuses on the details at the heart of every CV: your factsheet. This document is an unedited (and private) summary of your life. It will include everything about you from qualifications to employment history, from hobbies to how to get in touch.

Now is the time to verify that everything included in your factsheet is indeed <u>fact</u>.

- * Have errors crept into your contact details?
- * Where are the certificates for your qualifications?
- * Which month did you finish that employment?

Do it properly so you can be confident that your starting information is accurate.

You won't include the entire contents of this factsheet in every CV you send out, but it will form the foundation for all that follows.

Personal details

Name

Your CV should start with your name. Don't put 'Curriculum Vitae' or 'CV' at the top, because everyone knows what they're looking at. You don't write 'Shopping List' above a list of bread, milk, beans and toilet roll; your CV doesn't need to be labelled either.

The name you put doesn't have to be the full one from your birth certificate. Roger Winston Richard Johnson can just be Roger Johnson. If your first name is Christopher but everyone calls you Chris, put Chris. For a first name that is unusual, long, or often mispronounced, you might feel more comfortable using a shortened or anglicized version. This could be the name friends or colleagues normally call you.

Contact details

Standard practice is to list your:
* home address
* telephone number
* email address.

Address

State your full postal address, including an accurate postcode.

Telephone number

Be sure to include the area code and double check it is correct. Most recruiters will bin a CV if they dial the contact number and the person who answers has never heard of you.

For landlines, be clear which number you have given: work or home. The recruiter is less likely to leave an urgent message on a home number or expect you to call back the same day.

By including a work number, be prepared for calls at work. If you can' talk in front of others and no one knows you are considering leaving, it's best not to give this. Also, if you're sending your CV to a lot of places, you might get a lot of calls – which could tax the patience of the most understanding employer.

Try to stick to just one number if you can – it's far simpler and quicker for the person trying to contact you if there is only one option.

Mobile numbers are usually the best, as long as you have a signal during the day. If not, home numbers are better than work, but make sure your answering machine or voicemail works properly or your family know to take a message carefully. Getting home to find you've been invited to interview but no one can tell you when, or with whom, would be very frustrating. Be sure to check voicemail messages regularly.

If you will be sending your CV overseas, add the relevant international dialling code for your country.

Email

Choose your email address with care.

Will an employer cheer inwardly at the thought of employing facebookaddict@yahoo.co.uk, popmycherry@hotmail.com, thevodkamaster@googlemail.com or imabigloser@virgin.net?

If in any doubt, or you don't have an email address yet, it's easy to set up a free email account and choose a more professional-sounding address.

Try to keep your name the central focus of the address, even if you do have to include some numbers, and make it as simple as possible. anthonyperfect09@hotmail.com is infinitely better than 18756ii901lghif@hotmail.com: it's instantly clear who it belongs to, is less likely to be entered incorrectly, and probably won't be automatically classed as spam when you reply to a message.

Email addresses need to be as carefully checked as contact numbers when you type them. One letter or number out place and your invitation to an interview will end up in someone' else's inbox or lost forever in webspace. No recruiter or employer will try ten different versions of your email address to see if they land on the right one.

Personal information

Anti-discrimination law means you do NOT need to put these things on your CV:
* age or date of birth
* state of health

* gender
* race
* marital status
* sexual orientation
* number of dependants
* religious beliefs
* any other personal information.

Legal stuff aside, this kind of detail doesn't tell an employer anything useful anyway. Your focus should only be what you can offer them, and how well you can do the job.

Disability

Health and disability can be a grey area. You are under no obligation to mention any disability or health problems when applying for a job. However, you could disadvantage yourself if you don't. This is especially true if you need support to get your application in, or to access an interview.

Employers must provide reasonable support so anyone can compete for one of their jobs on an equal basis. Depending on your disability or illness, it could be worthwhile revealing relevant details in advance and requesting any specific help you may need. Even if you don't include it in your CV, you can say so in your covering letter.

Employers are allowed to ask candidates if they have a disability that might affect their ability to do the job they have applied for. But the employer also has to make any reasonable changes to the workplace that are needed for a disabled person to do the job as effectively as anyone else.

If you wish to keep your disability or ill health hidden, then that is your legal right. You are not obliged to admit or volunteer any information, even when asked directly. However, if your disability stops you from doing your job adequately at some point in the future, and you face losing your job, you can't fall back on the Disability Discrimination Act. This Act only protects those who actually tell an employer about their disability or ill health. If this issue affects you, it is worth getting further advice.

Security

From a personal security standpoint, it is not a good idea to send out any documents that contain your name, address, phone number *and* date of birth. This information alone is often enough for someone to commit identity fraud.

Unless you are asked to provide proof of UK residence with an application, such as a National Insurance number or your Passport number, never offer it on your CV. Normally it's enough to confirm you are a UK resident. Later in the recruitment process is when you might reasonably be asked to provide proof. Even if this proof is requested at the same time as your CV, you can send it in a separate letter or try phoning with the details.

Education

This step can be a bit disheartening if you are not overly proud of your education. Don't worry – if it isn't a star, it doesn't have to take centre stage.

First, ensure all your facts are correct. Find the original certificates and:

* Note down where you studied and when, including all the subjects, levels and grades.
* Include all your academic studies: GCSE, O Level, CSE, Standard, AS Level, A Level, Higher, BTEC, NVQ, City & Guilds, Baccalaureate, Bachelor's degree, Master's degree, PhD, etc.
* If you have studied beyond GCSE level (or CSE/O Levels), list your education in reverse date order: the highest level (i.e. most recent) education at the top of the list.
* Put the certificates together, labelled, where you can easily find them again.

It might seem like overkill to dig out original certificates, but there are two good reasons:

1 Accuracy

Even if your student years are not a distant memory, it's worth being sure that what you put down is 100 per cent correct. This is very important if you've been guilty of exaggeration on past CVs. Say something often enough and you can start to believe it yourself.

2 Proof

Any employer can ask for evidence of your qualifications, and at any time. Being unable to produce them can be embarrassing and frustrating, especially if your job offer relies on this proof. Getting copies can take a long time, assuming it's even possible.

Career, employment or work history

What you call this section depends on your viewpoint. After spending ten years in warehousing and distribution to become a logistics manager, or working your way up from kitchen hand to assistant head chef, 'Career History' works fine.

If you haven't been working long, or have jumped around from personal trainer to delivery driver to cruise ship entertainer, it's harder to say you've followed a career. 'Employment History' or 'Work History' might be more apt. It's really a matter of what you feel most comfortable with. Any of these titles makes it clear to the reader of your CV what they'll find in this section.

List whom you've worked for in a paid capacity: what role, when and for how long.

Just like Education, this section should be in reverse date order with your current or most recent job at the top.

Describe the company

If you've worked for a company that isn't well known, their name might not mean anything to the person reading your CV. Working as a manager for Megabucks for five years says nothing useful about you on its own.

But, when you add that Megabucks was:
* a new, fast-growing UK chain of coffee outlets, or
* a well-established family business importing moose hides from Canada, or
* a global manufacturer of high-tech money-printing machines

then the reader gets an instant picture. All of a sudden, they can imagine the kind of business environment you've worked in, even if they've never heard of the company.

If you're not sure how best to describe an employer, the 'About Us' section of their website is good for ideas. Try to keep the description to one line or so, and include these key details:

* industry: e.g. retail, importer, manufacturer
* products/services: e.g. coffee, moose hides, money-printing machines
* size: national, family, global
* status: established, new, market-leading, fast-growing, high tech, etc.

Your first job

School leavers and graduates are unlikely to have much to write here compared to someone who has worked for years, but this doesn't make any work experience less valid. You might want to avoid calling it your Career History though. Paid holiday roles, job shadowing and work experience are often better put under Work History or Work Experience.

Voluntary work

Just because it's unpaid doesn't mean it's unskilled or useless by any means. Voluntary work is not a poor cousin of paid work – it often uses many of the same skills, so don't be tempted to sweep it under the carpet. List any voluntary work you have done here, although for ease keep it in a separate section to your paid work.

If the voluntary work you have done is occasional rather than regular, you might prefer to include it in the Interests section instead.

Write what you did

Once you have your list of dates, companies and job titles, note exactly what you did in each job. Again, it's pure information you want at this stage, not something you'll present in a finished CV. Jot down as much as you can remember without trying to work out whether or not it sounds impressive. You can refine it later.

Your current or most recent job should be the easiest, so it's often best to start with that. If you get stuck, or can't think how to describe what you did, try answering a few of the questions below. Many job responsibilities involve working with one or more of the following:

* people
* money/finance
* systems
* thinking
* training/learning

Even if you're not stuck, these job responsibilities all require general skills that most employers are interested in, so they're a useful way to think about what you've done.

People

Does your job involve dealing with people?
If so:
* Do you do it in person, by phone or in writing (letter/email)?
* Are these people from your own company or other companies? From the media? Customers or members of the public?
* Do you serve or help these people, work with them as part of a team, negotiate with them, or manage them?

Try to mention:
* how often you dealt with people
* how many you dealt with
* who they were
* how you dealt with them.

Money/Finance

Do you deal with money in any way?
This could be:
* handling cash and/or credit card payments, cashing up
* bookkeeping, creating invoices

* selling goods and services, negotiating prices
* paying staff
* buying goods or services in from suppliers
* planning or managing a budget
* working out ways to save money or increase profits
* fundraising.

Many types of work give you some level of responsibility for money, or for profitability.

Any aspect of a job that includes money or finance is worth recording.

Systems

Do you use a system? Not just computers, but any kind of system:

* email, internet, intranet, or other office software/systems
* electronic tills, filing systems, stock control systems
* logistics, distribution tracking, warehousing systems
* accounts, invoicing, financial reporting, expenses, payroll, SAP
* planning, forecasting, ordering, project management systems
* design, engineering, CAD, print, manufacturing, etc.

It doesn't really matter which type of system you may use, the key thing is that you can learn and successfully use a system – and could learn to use a new system if needed, for a new employer.

Be sure to note down:

* how many/which systems you use
* whether the systems are universal or specific to this company
* how often you use it/them
* whether you help or train other people to use it/them.

Thinking skills

How much thought, judgement or decision making does your job need to be done well? For example, do you:

* solve problems for yourself, or colleagues or customers at work?
* come up with new ideas or design new things?

* think up simpler, faster, better or more efficient ways to do something?
* have to make decisions or judgements whilst at work?

Training/Learning

As well as doing your job, do you ever help or train other people?

This doesn't mean you have to be an official 'training manager', or even have 'training' in your job description. It might be something you do just because you are experienced, or because people are always asking you for help.

Whether a dedicated training manager or informal trainer or coach, try to note down:

* how many people you train or coach
* how often you train them
* who they are/what level i.e. colleagues/customers, juniors/peers/senior managers
* what you teach them
* why you are the person chosen/who volunteers to do it.

Professional qualifications and memberships

List the type, level and date of professional qualifications. Also, put the date and level of memberships of relevant organizations. For example:

* Member of the Chartered Management Institute since 2007
* 1995 – Member of the Royal Veterinary College
* 2009 Graduate Member of the Institute of Export (Associate Member since 2006)
* Student Member of the Institute of Civil Engineers (2008)

If you do not yet hold a relevant professional qualification but are working towards one, and are able to become a student or associate member, it may help to show a recruiter that you are serious about a career in the industry.

Further skills and training

This section covers qualifications or training courses that don't fall into the Education or Employment sections of your CV. What you call this depends on what you can include.

You might have taken further professional qualifications, specializing in a certain area or adding to your skills. These could be listed under 'Professional Development', for example:

* Microsoft or Cisco accreditation
* Quality Systems training
* Project Management qualifications.

Other recognized qualifications gained through external examinations can also be covered here, perhaps under a heading such as 'Further Skills':

* Secretarial: RSA Typing Level I and II, Pitman Shorthand
* Language: Chamber of Commerce French for Business, Certificado Inicial in Spanish as a Foreign Language
* Driving: HGV licence, Forklift licence
* IT: CLAIT (Computer Literacy And Information Technology)
* Culinary: Cordon Bleu
* Other: First Aid At Work, Food Hygiene, Nursery/Childcare, etc.

Other training courses could be specific to your employer or industry. How much you include in your final CV depends on how relevant it is: but at this stage try to write everything down.

Interests

Not everyone likes to include this section on their CV – and sometimes there may be good reasons not to – but for this initial step, note it all so it is not forgotten.

Things you can include in this section are:

* sports you teach, play or regularly support
* non-sporting clubs or teams you may be a member of: this could be the local carnival committee, film club, pub quiz team, history club, etc.

* other activities you enjoy regularly: street dance, quiz nights, skateboarding, off-road driving, stand-up comedy, theatre productions, barber shop group, learning to play an instrument, cookery lessons, etc.
* charity, community or voluntary work: fundraising event for a hospice, helping with a scout camp, reading to a blind friend, urban community project, hospital visiting, etc. This may take a more prominent position in your work history if you are currently out of work or are a school leaver with no other work experience.
* hobbies: tracing family history, restoring old cars, showing pedigree poodles, wildlife photography, silk painting, cake decorating, short story competitions, etc.

References

These generally aren't needed up front, but it's worth sorting out the details now.

Typically you need one professional and one personal reference, although this may vary depending on the role and industry. The professional one tends to come from a former employer (ideally the most recent), while the personal one can come from anyone who knows you well.

It pays to check in advance that someone is happy to be a referee for you, not least because you need to be sure that what they will say about you is appropriate – and positive. Being a referee can also take up quite a bit of time. You might apply for roles in several organizations and find that all want to see references before you receive any provisional job offers. When this happens, your referees may find themselves filling out lots of forms in a short space of time, and some can be very detailed.

Beware!

Employers have a lot to lose by employing dishonest employees. Fraud costs UK companies millions of pounds every day, and much of it is committed by employees, or with inside help. It's not hard to see why vetting new employees is something many take seriously.

Ensure that any references you do provide will stand up to scrutiny, warn your referees before they are contacted, and thank them afterwards.

2

what skills do you have?

Done properly, the Employment section of your CV should highlight your skills and show how they could benefit potential employers.

Time for a bit of self-analysis: a useful refresher if you know your skill set already, and essential if you're not quite sure what you have to offer an employer.

Every employer looks for certain skills and qualities that will make you useful to them, whatever your role. Most organizations love an employee who:

* does their own role well and can also take on new responsibilities
* communicates clearly and works well with other people
* is always trying to do things better.

This chapter walks you through the top ten 'generic' skills. It will help you to understand the kinds of skills you might be using at work and elsewhere, and where your strengths lie. This will prepare you for starting to talk about them in later chapters.

An ideal Employment section is a series of bullet points in which you show off your skills.

The key to doing this well is proof. Each bullet point must give some evidence that supports your claim to have these skills. We can all claim to be amazingly motivated, valuable, committed, skilled employees.

The moment you start coming up with examples to show that what you say is true, your CV starts to gather real power.

Building your Employment section

Starting with your most recent job in mind, try to answer the following three questions:

1 What did you actually do?

Don't rely too much on your job title to explain your past roles. What your job title says you do in your current company is often not the same at other companies you apply to.

Accurately note what you did/do for each company you've worked for, and at what level.

From the following list, note what you were/are handling:
* workload
* team sizes
* team complexity
* project deadlines
* budget sizes
* performance targets.

2 How well did you do what you did?

A CV that gives only a list of your job responsibilities doesn't say whether you did your job poorly, averagely or amazingly.

Old job descriptions can be a very handy reminder, but don't just copy them out word for word. Find proof: for each responsibility you mention, think of an example of how you showed you were good at it.

3 Do you still do what you did?

What you *actually* do now (or did when you left the job) can be very different from the official job description for the position you originally accepted.

If you stick to your old job description and title, you will be selling yourself short. Always be sure to describe what former jobs involved at their highest level.

What everyone wants

A great way to get into the right frame of mind for this next section is to think a bit more about what appeals to employers. Whatever kind of job you do or are looking for, there are certain 'generic' or transferable skills that most employers will value. The kinds of skills everyone wants.

Top ten generic skills

These skills are in no particular order:
* Communication
* Interpersonal skills
* Time management
* Problem solving
* Creativity and innovation
* Motivation
* Initiative
* Analytical skills
* Flexibility
* Negotiation

Communication

Communication is the ability to communicate information effectively to other people and receive it in return. It can be written, spoken or non-verbal.

Communication spans almost everything we do, and can include:
* answering telephones and taking messages
* writing anything from emails to a technical handbook

* contributing to a meeting
* interviewing someone
* public speaking
* training staff

Interpersonal skills (People skills)

In its most basic sense, this is the ability to get along with other people. At a higher level, it is being able to influence other people's mood and behaviour in a positive way.

Other ways you can demonstrate people skills is by being able to:
* calm down someone who is angry or upset
* use humour (appropriately!) to defuse tension
* give feedback while avoiding confrontation
* inspire and motivate a team to achieve their goals
* offer support and sympathy to someone in need.

Time management

Time management is being able to organize your time so you get through your tasks efficiently, while allowing time to handle any emergencies that might come up.

Problem solving

This is exactly what it says on the tin – solving problems. Almost everyone does this, at home or at work.

Not surprisingly, employers really appreciate people who come up with ways to help them carry out their business more efficiently and profitably, or in a more appealing or environmentally friendly way, all the while managing to keep customers happy.

Examples of solving problems include:
* Stopping soup tins jamming on a conveyor belt.
* Finding an alternative route that beats the traffic.
* Changing a filing system to save time looking for lost records.
* Coming up with a way to make an unprofitable product profitable.
* Devising a food and drink promotion to get enough customers in at lunchtimes.

Creativity and innovation

For CV purposes, being creative doesn't just have to mean you are brilliantly artistic. Creative or innovative thinking means approaching things from a new angle, seeing and doing things differently, finding links between different things or, in its most basic form, creating something new.

Creativity is often sparked by a desire to solve a problem or make improvements. You might have used your creativity when you:

* thought up a way to restock shelves faster or more efficiently
* worked out how to waste less cardboard when packaging products
* came up with a new product or service that no other company currently offers
* had a great idea for attracting more customers to the wine bar in the afternoon
* found a way to share advertising costs with retailers and increase sales together.

Motivation

All employers want to employ motivated staff: people whom they believe will work hard in the best interests of the company.

Motivation can be shown in many ways. It might be someone who:

* comes in a little early or leaves a little late to get a task finished
* gets their job done as fast and well as possible
* is keen to get involved in new projects
* thinks about a problem over the weekend, suggesting a solution on Monday
* takes on work beyond their job description to help the business succeed
* talks to customers with enthusiasm about company products or services
* gets people around them excited about the work that they do
* looks forward to their working day and to making a difference.

Initiative

An employee who spots something that needs to be done, and then does it without being asked, is showing initiative.

Most employers love this positive trait as they know that employees with initiative are not often sitting around unproductive. Whenever they are free, they will be looking for ways to benefit the business.

Analytical skills

This is looking at information in a logical way and, based on it, making a sensible decision. Analytical skills may sound advanced, but they are something we all use in our day-to-day lives.

You might read reports on ten different cars that you like the look of, take four for a test drive and then, based on the cost and what you feel you are getting for your money (trim, servicing, optional extras, finance) decide which is the best one to buy.

Flexibility

This is another trait that really appeals to employers – the ability (and willingness) to respond to changing situations. This might involve working in a different way, or learning new skills. 'Adaptability' is a term sometimes used instead of flexibility.

Covering for someone else while they are off sick, on holiday or on maternity leave, is often a way to show flexibility – perhaps you took on a different type of work, or increased your overall workload and delegated some of your work to someone else.

Negotiation

Negotiation is not about getting what you want. It's about working towards agreement: individuals, teams or companies with different aims finding a common solution that works for all parties.

You don't have to be a hostage negotiator or a buyer in a large company for negotiation to be a useful skill. Employers welcome this skill at every level.

If you are employed, the chances are you have done some sort of negotiation to gain your current role.

Convince an employer of your skills

The key to being convincing on your CV is not just to say which skills you have, but to show how you have used them.

Go back through each job in your factsheet, starting with your most recent job, and try to think of examples of how and when you have shown each of the ten skills.

Actions speak louder than words

When you think of examples, write down specific actions you have performed and results you have achieved. Focus on using verbs – action words – to describe them.

Explain what you did, made, suggested, improved, showed, tried or changed. Don't worry too much about which action word makes you sound best just yet. This is still your private factsheet, so just include as much detail as you can remember. You'll be refining it later on.

Don't ignore examples from outside work: these can prove useful in anyone's CV, but are particularly relevant for school leavers and graduates with little or no work experience, or for those returning from a career break.

Once you have thought of an example, put it into the right section of your factsheet: Employment or Work Experience, Education or Interests. If it is work related, make sure it is against the right company and the right job.

Specialist skills

Along with the generic skills listed above, there may be some specific or specialist skills and experience that you will need in order to do a job effectively. Some might be essential, others just an added bonus.

For any specialist skills you possess, go through the same 'proof' process as for your generic skills. Note down every example you can think of.

3

bringing out your best points

You've identified your valuable skills and made a list of examples to show when you've used them to good effect.

Depending on your experience, your list of skill examples may be long or short – it doesn't matter. What's important now is working out which examples deserve to go in your CV and how to put them across in the most convincing way.

Making a skill example convincing means including enough information to make it understandable and believable, while being concise enough for it to be read quickly. Fail on either count and the reader could doubt you or get lost in the detail.

To entice a recruiter to read your whole CV, your strengths should shine through as early as possible. This chapter also demonstrates how your best points can be combined into a brief summary right at the start.

What makes a good skill example?

For every example that you've noted, you need to check whether it is specific enough to add power to your CV. This next process, called SHORTlisting, will help you transform woolly examples into concise proof of your skills.

How do I SHORTlist my examples?

Every example needs to be as SHORT as it can be:
* **S**pecific: what exactly did you do, why and how?
* **H**onest: did <u>you</u> do it? Alone or as part of a team (what part did you play)?
* **O**utcome: was there a measurable result or benefit for your employer?
* **R**ealistic: does what you are claiming sound achievable – or like a fantasy?
* **T**ransferable: will this skill be useful to any future employer?
Let's take each aspect in turn.

Specific

Use details or numbers to explain exactly what you are talking about.

Honest

Do what it says on the tin: be honest.

Use an example only if it shows something you have actually done. Don't position yourself as having done something if you did not; nor should you take full credit for something you did as part of a team.

Outcome

This is one of the most essential pieces of information you can include: what difference your actions made to the company. This should ideally be measurable and could be:
* a sales or profit increase
* more customers coming through the door

* a reduction in wastage
* saving of time or money
* improvement in morale or relationships
* achievement of an award
* greater customer satisfaction
* more hits on a website, etc.

There may be some occasions when you simply can't put a figure to the difference that you've made: but you can often sensibly estimate one if you think about it.

Realistic

Put yourself in the shoes of the person reading your CV. Does the example you've used to demonstrate your skill sound realistic?

If it does, great. If it doesn't, check whether you have made a typing error or have overestimated, exaggerated or outright lied.

Transferable

Where your examples show generic skills, they should not need any further work. Generic skills are, by definition, transferable to any role and therefore useful to any employer.

However, you may also have examples of more specialist skills, which – unless you think laterally – may only be truly transferable if you are looking for work within the same field. Obviously for specialist skills, your example can only be SHOR at most. The same example could if necessary be tweaked to show off a different skill, one that is more relevant.

Starting with your own examples

The quick way to check how strong your examples are is to note an S, H, O, R and T against each one if it definitely meets that requirement.

You may, after going through all parts of this process, find you just can't make an example properly **SHORT**. Despite your best efforts, it is still missing one or more areas. Don't discard it: just mark clearly the areas it does meet, such as **SHRT**, and move on.

At the end, you may find it's still the best example you can come up with for that skill. Once you've SHORTlisted all your examples, the best ones to use for each CV you write will be obvious.

Prioritizing the essentials

It's time to understand just what an employer is going to do with your CV. To do that, you need to know who is reading your CV – or at least, what is important to them.

Whoever reads your CV will be working under two main constraints: time and knowledge.

Time constraints

Most people are under time constraints at work; no one is ever going to take as much time to read your CV as you hope they will. This can seem unfair given the effort you are going to, but if you make it easy for someone to quickly see why you should be shortlisted for interview (or why your CV shouldn't go in the bin), then all the effort will have been worth it.

To suit time constraints, your CV needs to be **brief** and **relevant**.

Knowledge constraints

The other thing to keep in mind is that the first people to read your CV may not be those you will be interviewed by or end up working for.

To account for these knowledge constraints, your CV needs to use plain English – ideally no jargon unless it is specifically mentioned in the job advertisement.

Start as you mean to go on

Your skill examples, properly SHORTlisted, will be brief, relevant and in plain English. That's good.

They are also buried in your Employment History. Not so good.

How can you make sure someone so short of time reads enough of your CV to make sure they see all these brilliant examples? You can't. But you can make it easy for them by giving your highlights at the start.

Exactly what you call it is up to you. If in doubt, something simple such as Summary, Profile or Key Skills is probably the safest option. Using the word 'Professional' is probably inappropriate if you have little or no work experience or you don't work in a professional field.

Converting SHORTlisted examples into a summary

Two simple steps will create your Summary:

1 Decide which five skills are your priorities.
2 Select your best example bullet points.

Priorities

The five skills you choose should closely match the job description or the general field you are applying for. If you don't have a job advert in mind, are preparing your CV well in advance, or want to think about a new direction, you will probably need to revisit this later when creating your CV for a specific job application.

Select your bullet points

Go through your employment history and pull out all the bullet points that demonstrate the five skills you have prioritized. Pick the single strongest, **SHORT**est example for each of the five skills.

Now you have two options. You can edit them into:

* a brief bulleted list
* a short prose summary.

Which option you choose is down to you. Some people stick to bullets all the way; others like to vary their CV style by alternating prose and bullet points. Provided the end result still contains specific evidence to support your claims, it really doesn't matter.

Bulleted summary

If you decide on a bulleted list:
* keep it brief: it's called 'highlights' for a reason
* don't waste CV space by repeating yourself word for word.

Advantages

Bulleted lists are quick and easy to scan through.

Disadvantages

Almost all your CV will be bullet points, making it harder for different sections to stand out.

It's harder to show any sense of personality in bullet points.

Prose summary

If you decide on a prose summary:
* combine and edit your examples into three or four sentences at most
* ensure you retain concrete proof for at least your two best skills
* include in your Employment section any specifics you had to edit out.

Advantages

It varies the layout of your CV, making it easy to distinguish between different sections.

Prose makes it easier to inject a little of your personality into the summary.

Disadvantages

Starting a CV with a prose profile or summary may be more of a risk, as so many are done poorly and sound identical. Some recruiters have become cynical about prose profiles and so may give them less weight, but keeping proof of your skills at the core of your summary should overcome their prejudice.

Once you've completed your edited bullets or three sentences of prose, that's the first draft of your Profile or Summary done. Don't worry if it doesn't sound quite finished yet: as usual, you will be refining it later anyway so will have a chance to revisit it.

Add your highlights at the top of your factsheet, underneath your personal details. Your factsheet should now be starting to look like a basic CV.

4

using effective language

Your factsheet is now filled with facts, skills and supporting examples. Your skill examples have been SHORTlisted, prioritized, and also combined to create an opening summary to entice the reader. Your factsheet has become your 'generic CV'.

Like the factsheet, a generic CV is also a private document: one from which you will ultimately create every tailored CV you send. But before you reach that stage, you need to do something further to increase the impact: refine your language.

Refining is about choosing words and phrases that will 'lift' your CV from the pile. Effective language can help you stand out above people with similar – or even better – experience and skills to your own.

This chapter highlights the importance of powerful, action-oriented and evidence-based words and gives some useful examples. If you've already written your CV, this is a good opportunity to check and refine your language.

Effective language to make you stand out

How you approach this aspect of CV writing depends largely on how you feel about language.

Some people deliberately ignore this stage: they feel confident that their concrete achievements and proven abilities speak for themselves, and don't appreciate how essential good writing is.

Others simply don't understand what this part involves and therefore can't see why it is so important.

The basic rules of CV writing

There are three basic points that it helps to understand before you start:

1 The most critical words on your CV are those you start each section or bullet point with. These will be the first – and possibly the only – words read by an employer or recruiter who quickly scans through your CV. They should be verbs – action words.

2 The words you use to describe yourself speak volumes about you as a person. This is especially true of the verbs – or action words – that you include in your CV.

3 Impressive words or 'management speak' are not the foundation of a well-written CV. Just think carefully about the words you choose and, in some cases, try stretching yourself a little bit further than might normally feel comfortable.

Why action words matter

The most important words in your CV will be your action words. This is partly because all examples in your Employment section should begin with action words, and partly because these are the words that show employers what you are capable of **doing**.

How you describe what you've done – or what you can do – will make a huge difference to how they perceive you, your abilities, and even your whole attitude to work.

Refining your action words

With this in mind, check your CV factsheet for the skill examples in your Employment section. These bullet points should all have action words at or very near the beginning, which describe what you were doing in that role.

Look carefully at these action words: have you used the best possible one to describe what you did? If it could give the wrong impression about you, think of another way to put it. Most 'standard' action words have one or more 'power' alternatives to try instead.

Finding the right word to use is all about balance. Your CV is, after all, about you. Sometimes you'll feel more comfortable with a straightforward action word than the power alternative, especially if the power alternative is a word you:

* would never normally say
* are not comfortable pronouncing
* feel is a bit too strong to describe what you actually did.

Power action words

On the other hand, there is nothing wrong with making the very most of everything you've done; in many cases, there is more than one alternative you can consider.

Examples

Basic   Coming up with a business plan
                              Writing a business plan

There is nothing wrong with coming up with good ideas, although it can suggest it was a bit of a spur of the moment thing. If all you did was write it, does that mean someone else told you what to put?

Power alternatives   Building a business plan
                              Creating a business plan
                              Devising a business plan

Built it from scratch, created something, devised something brilliant … all these sound more impressive and more personally responsible for the outcome.

Basic	Changing a system

This doesn't mention whether things were better after your change … or even whether the change was deliberate.

Power alternatives	Improving a system
	Overhauling an entire system
	Upgrading a system

You improved one or more aspects, overhauled the whole thing, upgraded to a better version … all these alternatives suggest a much more positive action and result.

Basic	Answering the telephone

So … do you put it down again without saying a word? HOW do you answer it?

Power alternatives	Representing the company by answering all incoming calls
	Creating a positive first impression for all callers

If you work on reception or switchboard and put external calls through, using words like these can show that you realize how important a good first impression can be to a company's reputation.

If you do something as a result of answering the telephone, focus on what you do:

Power alternatives	Dealing with customer enquiries
	Handling customer enquiries
	Resolving customer enquiries

These suggest you are actively taking charge of your telephone calls and make you sound more like a problem solver.

Present vs. past tense

For your action verbs you can use one of two tenses:

* Doing (present tense)
* Did (past tense)

It's up to you which you use.

The present tense can make older skills and examples sound more current, helping your entire CV to feel more dynamic.

However, another school of thought favours the past tense. The reasoning behind this is that writing:

* **Devising** innovative business plans

instead of

* **Devised** innovative business plans

could suggest to some people that you haven't yet developed that particular skill and are still working on it, instead of having mastered it successfully.

Both approaches are equally valid: select whichever tense you feel most comfortable using. But take care to stick to the tense you choose – and double check it stays the same throughout your CV.

Refining your adjectives

Adjectives, or description words, are another way to turn a standard role or activity into something special. They help the reader to compare you positively against other people who appear to have a similar history to your own.

Example

Let's say you are in sales and up against hundreds of other salespeople for the job of account manager at another company. Describing yourself as 'leader of a sales team' won't make you stand out from this crowd. It could be any sales team you're talking about – maybe even the worst one in the country.

Better, you could be ...

* leading an **award-winning** sales team
* contributing to the most **successful** sales team ever

* the **fastest** closer in the telesales team
* the third **highest grossing** salesperson in the division
* voted **top** salesperson by the Sales and Marketing department three years running
* the second most **successful** salesman of 2008
* the **only** account manager **never to have lost a customer**
* the **leading** commission earner in the sales department
* the **first** to make a sale in the on licence sector.

You'll notice that these words (in bold) are not only positive but specific and measurable. This indicates that what you are saying has substance. Even if you don't say in your CV what award your 'award-winning team' managed to achieve, the mere mention of it invites someone to interview you and find out more.

Another way to achieve the same effect and make it clear that you can back up your claim with evidence is to talk about yourself using the following kinds of phrases:
* '**proven** negotiator'
* '**strong track record** in selling to retail'
* '**demonstrable** communication skills'
* '**award-winning** designer'.

However you supply the proof, referring to it in a specific and measurable way adds a great deal of power to your CV.

Avoid repetition

Power words quickly lose their strength and impact if they are repeated too often.

By varying the words that you use, you help to give all your adjectives more power.

Reducing word count, not power

Four ways to keep things brief but still powerful include:
* writing in note form, not full sentences
* avoiding repeating words and phrases

* not telling people something they already know
  (or can safely assume)
* keeping in specific details that make your skills stand out.

Good
* **Selling** high value oxygen monitors.
* **Working** with private and NHS nurses, consultants and paramedics.
* **Demonstrating** equipment to medical staff.

Better
* **Selling** new, high value oxygen monitors successfully.
* **Forming relationships** with private and NHS nurses, consultants and paramedics.
* **Communicating product benefits** while training groups of ten medical staff.

Best
* **Beating annual sales target** by 10 per cent in 2009.
* **Successfully positioning** new, high value oxygen monitors as essential equipment.
* **Building lasting relationships** with private/NHS consultants, paramedics and nurses.
* **Reinforcing product benefits** while single-handedly training staff in groups of ten.

true lies – marketing or deceit?

CVs allow you to showcase your talents in a way that entices a prospective employer. That's what a recruiter expects when they ask to see your CV. If you don't exploit this opportunity to market yourself in whatever way you like, you will miss out.

A CV is a great marketing tool because you can steer the content in any direction you wish. You are permitted, even encouraged, to focus only on the information that best supports your application. Less positive aspects can often be left out.

The one thing you should never do on your CV is include something that isn't true, however small. It's easy to convince yourself that every other candidate who applies for the role is perfect and therefore you need to lie. They aren't, and you don't.

This chapter prompts you to think about the differences between marketing and misrepresentation, and to consider the implications.

However well you present your skills and achievements in a positive light, there will probably still be areas of your CV where you wish you had something better to say. It can be very tempting, when looking at these less impressive parts of your CV, to make something up. But the only possible advice for someone in this situation is: **Don't**.

Education lies

Let's say you lie about your grades or qualifications. They don't quite meet the job spec or aren't something you feel proud of. What happens when you are asked for evidence? Where would a certificate come from ... or could you sit a test to prove your knowledge?

Lies are not just when you claim to have something that you don't – exaggeration is also a form of lying. You don't feel proud of your 2.2 in English from Bristol University so you bump it up – just a little – to a 2.1. Or maybe you say you got your degree from Cambridge University instead, as you had a girlfriend there.

How could you possibly be found out? Lots of ways:

* An interviewer who studied English at Cambridge themselves and wants to know which tutor you had.
* A chance search on Facebook, where you clearly show as part of the Bristol University network.
* A pre- (or post-) interview screening by a professional screening company in which your university attendance and results are verified.

Employment lies

When you lie about a former job or exaggerate your responsibilities, what happens when your prospective employer ... contacts your old boss? ... Googles you and finds an old web page showing your real job title? ... asks the professional screening company to make a few calls?

Other lies

There may be some areas of your CV where you think you are quite safe to lie. Little lies, because you can't possibly get caught – not even by the professionals. A more interesting-sounding interest; elevating your spoken Spanish from tourist to business level; several months' travel abroad to cover up that inconvenient gap in your employment.

If an untruthful CV does get you to interview, can you carry through your lies convincingly? You could be challenged in any number of ways, not just at interview but in future:

* You add yoga as an interest: your interviewer turns out to be a Hatha Yoga instructor.
* You claim advanced spoken German: the HR manager spent a year in the Munich branch (or married a German) and happens to speak it fluently.
* You add 'six months' backpacking in Vietnam', thinking it an unusual destination, but end up face to face with someone who toured South East Asia during their gap year.
* You mention abseiling as a hobby, but then refuse to go near a climbing wall during your first corporate event, citing your lifelong fear of heights.

What's the worst that can happen?

If you do decide to go the untruthful route, you will have to see it through to the end, one way or another. Frequently, the end is not good.

Not everyone can be a Lee McQueen, the winning contestant on the 2008 series of BBC TV's *The Apprentice*. McQueen lied about his education on his CV, got caught out during an interview, and yet *still* got the job. The boardroom explanation for this unusual decision was that McQueen was believed to have lied simply because he wanted the job so much – and that this level of eagerness was actually a positive thing. In fact, most employers do not appreciate this kind of eagerness; they prefer integrity.

Being caught in one lie, even if it is a 'small' one, will cast doubt on everything else that you claim in your CV. If it really is that small a lie, why bother with it, especially if it could cancel out all the genuine skills you offer?

Lying on your CV to get a job is considered by most employers to be gross misconduct. This can lead to instant dismissal, whether they find out about the lie on day 1 or day 1000 of your new job.

When does a stretch become a lie?

Only you know when a slight exaggeration of your skills and abilities tips the scales and becomes a lie. If your moral compass tells you that you're pushing it, or the thought of being challenged or asked for detail makes you at all nervous, don't put it in your CV.

What if I'm just not good enough?

As a rule, always apply for jobs you are qualified and competent to do. However, that doesn't mean you should assume you aren't good enough or that an employer won't consider you for a particular job just because you don't meet every single one of their requirements. There is usually a mix of essential and nice-to-have skills listed on any job advert. Provided you meet the essential requirements, don't be put off if you don't have every nice-to-have skill or quite as many years of experience as they are asking. If you want to operate on sick patients you obviously need surgical qualifications but for many jobs you can often succeed by selling the skills and experience you do have because an employer may still appreciate what you can offer.

As long as you are being realistic about your ability to do the job in question, it's worth applying.

Do I have to be honest about everything?

Every claim you make in your CV must be truthful. However, there is no rule that says you have to mention absolutely everything.

Some omissions will arouse suspicion. Unexplained gaps in employment are rarely ignored. Glaring omissions will result in detailed questions at interview (best case) or could just mean your CV gets junked right from the start (worst case), so you will need to find a way to handle these.

If I can't lie, what can I do?

Taking the honest approach doesn't mean all your warts have to be on display. Most problem areas can be successfully dealt with by what can be called 'honest spin'.

6

handling problem areas

If you accept the premise put forward in Chapter 5 (that lying is a bad idea), how do you handle any problem areas on your CV? The most common are breaks in employment and health issues.

Misdirection is a useful technique: focusing strongly on your positive aspects, as shown in Chapter 3, automatically draws attention away from areas you're less proud of.

Deletion is another option: try cutting the things you don't like from your generic CV. Sometimes it's that simple – but it can also leave huge unexplained gaps that the reader may fill with something worse than the truth.

A very useful technique, both for CV writing and interviews, is 'honest spin'. This acknowledges unfortunate events and circumstances but supplies a positive interpretation. The more positively you think about your CV, the easier it is to get a recruiter to agree with you and this chapter shows you how.

Just as Max Clifford does for his clients through clever PR, being careful with your words can help transform a lacklustre CV into something everyone wants to read.

The trick is to find a way to make people focus on what *you* want them to focus on.

Generally speaking, it's best not to bring up a problem area if it can be avoided: you are perfectly entitled to be picky about what you include in your CV. Some things will need explanation though, or your reader could end up making assumptions that are much worse than reality. For this, you can use honest spin.

Honest spin doesn't lie about an issue; instead it acknowledges it but focuses on the positive. So, what kind of problems can be tackled using honest spin?

Gaps in employment

Employment gaps can happen to anyone, and can be caused by a number of things:

* voluntary or involuntary redundancy
* sabbatical
* long-term illness
* being fired
* career break to raise a family or care for a relative
* retraining
* being a school leaver or university graduate
* a prison sentence
* travel
* resigning after making a poor career move.

Any of the above can see you out of work for some time. While many do not actually reflect on your ability to do a job, most employers still see being out of work as negative.

Mind the gap

Shorter gaps of a few weeks or months can sometimes be smoothed over by mentioning only the years (not the years and months) that you worked for an employer. It's an effective way to avoid focusing on any gaps, but because of this some recruiters may automatically view with suspicion any CV that gives only the years of employment.

Longer gaps, or gaps that happen to span two calendar years, tend to look more obvious and it's rather awkward to handle them this way.

Depending on the reason for the gap, it is often better to include a brief explanation rather than leave the reader to fill in the blanks themselves. Chances are you can explain the reasons better and more positively than their imagination will. Volunteering a brief explanation for an employment gap can make you seem a more attractive prospect as it shows you are honest, which sensible employers value highly.

Another way to distract recruiters from a gap is to change the format of your CV so that your skills examples are given before your employment history and dates. This is called a functional CV and will be covered in more detail in Chapter 8.

Temporary employment

Having gaps in between work and jumping around from company to company is par for the course if you do temporary work. This doesn't automatically reflect badly upon you, and some employers value the kind of experience and skills this type of work can bring.

To avoid someone making the wrong assumption, it can be worth adding a couple of lines to introduce your temp status before getting into dates.

Example

Range of office-based temporary administration positions gained through two principal agencies. Always in demand and often requested for repeat assignments.

If you have done temp work for a long time or for a lot of different employers, you can group your employers, skills and achievements to make clearer what you have to offer.

While leaving information out of your CV is not lying, it doesn't mean you can forget about it or pretend it never happened. If at interview you are asked directly whether you have ever made a bad job move, or have ever spent time out of work, then you should answer honestly.

Be prepared to explain your past in a positive light. By all means say that you left it off your CV because you didn't feel it added anything to your capabilities. By giving it proper thought beforehand, it won't come as such a shock to be asked the question – and you won't be tempted to try to lie when put on the spot.

How to use honest SPIN

When explaining something on your CV, from employment gaps to unfinished courses, it helps to follow a few simple rules. Keep it:

* **S**hort
* **P**ositive
* **I**nformative
* **N**atural.

Short

Don't take pages to give every last detail of your situation. Stay brief and to the point.

Positive

Think about how you can make this potential 'problem' sound like a good thing. If that's not possible, try to:

* Make it appear neutral instead of detrimental.
* Point out that it does not diminish what you can offer an employer.
* Demonstrate skills gained or opportunities taken as a result.

Informative

While keeping it short, do ensure you include any details necessary to avoid confusion.

Natural

If this is the first time you have tried to explain something in a positive light, make sure you feel comfortable with it and that it will hold up under scrutiny. Your explanation should feel natural, and you need to be convincing when discussing it. If you don't believe it, no one else will.

The four rules of honest **SPIN** apply to any explanation you may give, whether in an application form, a covering letter or even at interview.

Work on your positive story

Problem 1: An employment gap after redundancy

You were made redundant at very short notice along with 30 colleagues when your struggling employer had to shut down an entire division. The redundancy came as a surprise to all of you, but it took almost nine months to find your next role. How do you explain this big a gap in a positive way?

The answers to these three points are the basis of your explanation.

1 Redundancy is about luck – bad luck – and not about skill. It can hit anyone at any time and if you're really unlucky, more than once. But it's important to see – and believe – that being made redundant is no reflection on your skills or abilities.

2 If you were made redundant suddenly, it can be easier to justify a longer gap as you had no time to start a job search before leaving. If you took voluntary redundancy or had plenty of warning, how quickly did you jump into action, or did you do something else before focusing on your job search? What did you do, and did this gain you any skills?

3 In general, what have you done while unemployed? Learned any new skills? Done any training courses, voluntary or charity work, computer courses, learned a language, started your own business, coached a junior football team, renovated your house? Focus on the routine you've kept, activities you've done, what you've learned and what you can offer, not on the fact you weren't in paid work.

Now you're thinking positively, the entry on your CV could look like this:

Jan 2007–Nov 2007   **Volunteer Fundraising and Events Co-ordinator, RSPU**

* Focusing on enhancing interpersonal and communication skills after redundancy.
* Raising more than £25,000 in just nine months with a team of three volunteers.
* Building a network of relationships with local business people to raise the charity's profile.
* Organizing events such as a memorable three-legged 'horse' race through the town centre.

If you didn't do any kind of work but did training instead, focus on what you've learned in the same way:

Jan 2007–Nov 2007   **Skills development**

* Broadening my computing, financial and language skills following redundancy.
* Gaining CLAIT qualification, experience setting up macro-based Excel reporting.
* Enhancing budget management skills by studying accounting and bookkeeping.
* Learning to speak Spanish as a foreign language – awarded Elementary certificate.

Reason for leaving

Your CV is simply not the place to discuss your reasons for leaving. If these do need to be addressed, do it at interview – indeed it is quite common to be questioned on why you changed roles or why you are looking for a job now – but don't give the information up front. It won't add to your appeal, especially if you were fired.

Employer criticism

If you bad mouth a former employer (even if it is wholly justified in your view), it can suggest that you are a difficult personality. A reader could see you as a complainer, someone who will fall out with your next employer – and possibly end up talking about them negatively as well.

Employment tribunals

Don't mention tribunals unless asked. However justified, and however successful the result, you may still come across as the kind of person prepared to fight your employer through legal proceedings – something that many employers are understandably wary of.

If you do have to tackle the subject, do it at interview and discuss the facts calmly and positively. Focus on what you can offer an employer and what you look for in an ideal role, rather than on what hasn't worked in the past or what you don't like.

Illness

Problem 2: Long-term illness

Several years ago I was diagnosed with bipolar disorder and was prescribed medication. I stopped taking the medication when I was made redundant and then suffered an acute episode which resulted in three months' hospitalization.

A combination of therapy and new medication settled everything down and I felt back to normal, and was able to find another job through a friend. I'm now looking for my next move. Do I have to mention any of this in my CV, as I spent a total of six months off work?

It's simplest if, by the time of writing your CV, your illness is over and you have completely recovered. If your past illness or current condition won't affect your ability to do this new job – and you have your doctor's agreement on this – it's worth explaining, but very briefly.

Of course the type of job you apply for needs to be appropriate to your circumstances. If you are a qualified mechanic now unable to do physical work, you might not cut it as a mechanic but could bring unparalleled technical knowledge to the role of parts manager, service manager or new car salesman at a dealership. If both you and your doctor are confident you are capable to do this work, you apply for the right role, and you sell your skills in the right way, then you become an attractive prospect despite any illness.

Proof

Nervous about starting work again or feel that employers won't believe you when you say you are capable of doing the job? Consider starting work experience or voluntary work to demonstrate your fitness. Depending on the nature of your illness, this may also be a good way to ease yourself back into full-time work, and could give you some recent skill examples to include in your CV.

Disability

If an illness has left you with a long-term limited ability to do certain tasks, this is effectively a disability. In this case, think carefully about what to disclose on your CV or application and during interview.

Mentioning a disability isn't compulsory. If it isn't obvious, it might be very tempting to keep it quiet. But bear in mind that if you do not warn your employer, and you end up unable to do your job properly because of your disability, you can legally be dismissed for poor performance if your employer isn't aware you are disabled.

When mentioning any disability, your CV focus should still be putting a positive spin on what you are able to do unaided, and what further value you can add if the employer makes reasonable adjustments to support you. Never focus on what you can't do.

Mind your language

When it comes to honest spin, the language you use is all-important. Words can bring all sorts of images into an employer's mind: make sure these images are positive.

Negative

* Unemployed
* Out of work

Neutral

* Looking for work
* Finding a new job

Positive

* Researching jobs
* Evaluating alternatives
* Considering options
* Planning your next move

The more active and in control you can make yourself sound, whatever your situation, the more positive you will appear to an employer.

jargon – include, explain or avoid?

This chapter is particularly relevant if you are changing career or industry. Jargon is effectively a different language: if you don't speak it, then it means nothing to you.

You wouldn't send your CV in French to a British employer, *n'est-ce pas*? Not unless the job advert was in French, perhaps, or clearly requested a French CV.

The same applies to jargon. Starting with the job advert, try to reflect the employer's or recruiter's frequency and level of jargon.

Some people are fond of jargon and feel it shows they have expertise in their field, yet overuse can make a CV incomprehensible. Others hate jargon and avoid it studiously, even though universally accepted jargon can save valuable space and time on your CV.

Work through this chapter to help you establish an appropriate level of jargon for each application.

What is jargon?

Jargon consists of words, brands, acronyms, abbreviations and expressions with specific meanings. It can be industry-specific, company-specific, technical or generic and it is almost always used as a kind of shorthand. Jargon allows you to refer to something in an agreed way that your colleagues should understand. Most people use jargon in their everyday speech at work and, while some jargon is fairly specialized, much is so widely used that it becomes commonplace.

Whether you enjoy using – or reading – jargon is a very personal thing. Even if it's something you dislike, it can be tempting to use lots of jargon in your CV simply because it's a great way to save space. But at the initial stage of the recruitment process – or at any stage of it – you have no control over who might read your CV. It could be a specialist, but it could equally be an HR executive with little or no understanding of the specific role you are applying for. So, use jargon as little as possible.

Rules for jargon

Take the same tone as the employer

Boundaries for the amount and type of jargon you can safely use are typically set by the advert for the job you are applying for.

When it includes some jargon, you can fairly safely repeat those terms in your CV; indeed you may need to in order for recruiters or scanners to pick up these key words.

For more plainly worded adverts, try to avoid using any jargon at all or – if you have to use some – give an explanation.

If you are applying speculatively to a company and have no advert to refer to, check their website and any other job vacancies they are advertising to see how much jargon is used in their external communications.

Know your audience

Addressing your CV to an HR department or a recruitment agency means limit your jargon to essentials only, unless you are using key words from their advert.

If the CV should be sent to the manager of the department you would be working for, greater use of jargon is probably acceptable but ensure it is universally understood.

If you don't know who your CV will be read by, always minimize jargon.

Applying within the same industry

For a new role in the same industry, any industry-wide technical jargon will probably be understood by your future employer.

However, remember your CV may start with an HR audience so ensure you don't use any more than you need, and that sentences still make sense to someone who doesn't know the technical terms.

Applying to a new industry

If you are after a change of direction, chances are the industry you apply to will not know or understand the previous field you worked in. In this case remove all industry jargon or, if not possible, provide an explanation.

This can be particularly relevant for military personnel applying for civilian jobs. The military is famous for its extensive jargon, much of which is essential to understanding. However, it creates a real minefield when it comes to de-jargonizing your CV. It helps if you 'translate' your CV: this means focusing on your transferable skills above everything else, and ensuring your relevant skill examples are carefully described in plain English.

Technical considerations (for example, IT)

In some fields, use of jargon is almost a prerequisite; IT is one of them. If you don't mention the software or programming jargon appropriate to your level, it may be assumed – rightly or wrongly – that you don't have the knowledge or experience you claim.

However, you still need to pass the understandability test. Even if someone doesn't know the particular acronym you are using, it should at least be possible to figure out that it is software, for example.

Being concise vs. clear

Yes, jargon can help to keep the word count down. However, this shouldn't be at the expense of getting clear messages across in your CV.

Feedback: The acid test

When in doubt, ask a colleague in your industry and a friend who is totally unrelated to it to give you feedback on your CV. Ask them to be totally honest and to say any parts they didn't understand. If it makes sense to both of them, you have probably got your jargon balance about right.

Job titles

Example

Candidate applying for the Production Manager's role in a printing factory:

* 11 years managing packaging and corrugate production, leading teams of 80 people
* controlling CAD and CTP, all print types, corrugation and finishing
* devising innovative process solutions to reduce customer lead times by up to 20%
* successfully implementing ISO 900123 and BS 3456 compliance on three sites
* introducing Bobst Mistral AcuBraille machine for pharmaceutical packaging in 2009.

Same candidate applying for the Production Manager's role in a food factory:

* 11 years' production management experience with teams of 80 people
* successfully introducing industry quality standards on three different sites
* devising innovative ways to reduce customer lead times by up to 20%

> *   staying competitive with clever equipment purchasing:
>   e.g. winning new orders with AcuBraille (automated
>   Braille embossing machine) for pharmaceutical
>   customers.
>
> On the surface of it, the second version doesn't sound all that
> different from the first, but it should make far more sense to
> someone with no experience of the printing industry.
>
> Check that losing the jargon doesn't make your CV less specific:
> where necessary, as in the final point above, you can briefly explain
> jargon instead of deleting it.

Loosely, the rules of jargon also apply to job titles. A supervisor
in a coal mine may have a totally different type of role to a supervisor
in a factory, or a supervisor in a telesales department. An account
manager in one company may have a vastly different remit to an
account manager in another.

So, like jargon, don't rely on job titles to bring instant
understanding to your audience. This is another reason why it
is so important to include your specific achievements and to
demonstrate your level of skill in your Employment section.

8

being specific — targeting your CV

It's worth repeating: the generic CV that you've compiled over Chapters 1–7 should *never* be sent out as it stands. A generic CV that was designed for all is suited to none. That's why you should never print multiple copies of the same CV: each one should be unique.

The previous chapter hinted at taking a different approach for every application. From here on in, this is the single most important aspect of CV preparation: targeting it effectively. That means targeting a specific industry or sector, a specific company within that sector, and a specific role within that company.

If you have time for nothing else, this is the chapter you should read. Always do your research; make sure your story is strong; and only ever send out a properly targeted CV.

Creating a targeted CV from your generic CV, which may be much longer, means selecting the most relevant and powerful material to put in your one to two pages.

If you are unsure about what is required in a particular CV, bear in mind that a powerful, concise two-pager never offended anyone. However, it helps if your CV is appropriately constructed for the sector you are applying to and includes all the relevant details an employer would normally expect to see.

Understand what the sector expects

Ask yourself what you will be doing, and what kinds of skills and knowledge are most likely to be valued. You can't tailor a CV effectively unless you know what is desirable.

Be genuinely enthusiastic about the field you are trying to get into

If railways are your passion, make sure it is clearly demonstrated in your CV when you apply for that job as a track maintenance technician or rail customer service adviser.

Genuine enthusiasm will help you stand out from a crowd of applicants who are simply desperate for any job as a technician or in customer service. Or just any job.

Most companies want to attract and retain loyal employees. It's a far safer bet to recruit someone who'd love to work in their industry and who can show them why.

Lengths of specialist CVs

Despite your best efforts, there will be some things you cannot fit onto two pages. These might cover:
* publications and lectures for a long-standing academic
* schools worked at for an experienced supply teacher
* complete project list for a long-qualified engineer
* all procedures performed by a consultant neurosurgeon
* an account of all a diplomat's research and policy recommendations.

This doesn't mean you can ignore relevance and brevity. It will still benefit you to select the most recent and meaningful examples.

If your aim when supplying this information is to show breadth or depth of experience, you can still refer to the quantity/scope of your work while listing only the highlights. Where full and specific details are requested, though, you will need to supply these. However, you could provide these in a supplement or appendix (as you might do with references) and therefore still leave your main CV powerfully concise.

Which type of CV to use

There are three main accepted CV formats:
* chronological (reverse chronological)
* functional
* hybrid (combination of chronological and functional).

Chronological

The standard, most common CV type is the reverse chronological, which has everything in reverse date order. Up until this point, reverse chronological has been assumed because recruiters are more familiar with this than any other type. Provided a reverse chronological CV is well written, recruiters should be able to see easily if someone has the evidence and experience they seek.

Pros and cons
* All recruiters are very familiar with the format.
* It's quick to scan through.
* Your CV is easy to compare side by side with others.

But ...
* If your employment history is not great, it can be harder to do yourself justice.

Should you deem reverse chronological unsuitable for your circumstances or for a particular application, alternative formats do exist.

Functional

Given that content and layout should be relevant to the industry, company and job you are applying for, a functional CV might help display your talents more appropriately. This focuses on what you can **do**, based on the sum total of your experience.

Functional CVs don't list achievements and examples of skills in date order, by job or by employer. Instead they start by highlighting the most useful and transferable knowledge and skills that you offer, some career- or industry-specific and others more generic.

A functional CV format can work well if:

* your specialist experience is key
* you are changing career or industry
* you are applying for very senior positions
* you are a graduate or school leaver with little or no work experience
* you have had numerous different jobs, each for a short space of time
* your work is project-based in nature
* your work experience and/or knowledge spans more than one industry.

Depending on the field you apply for, a functional CV can work better than a chronological CV. If your skills and experience were gained through a long series of projects or assignments, the sum of what you can offer a future employer will carry more weight than a long list of past employers or projects.

Functional CVs are by no means common in many sectors, although they shouldn't be totally alien to any major recruiters.

Pros and cons

* Clear summary of the skills you offer: recruiters don't have to dig for details.
* Your functional competencies are obvious without reading your Employment section.
* Clusters lengthy or varied work and projects.
* Can help make your CV more concise.

But ...

* Some recruiters may be suspicious you are trying to conceal employment gaps.
* Recruiters unused to this format may find it more difficult to scan quickly.
* Can be harder to compare against reverse chronological CVs.

Hybrid

For the truly undecided, there is a third option called a hybrid CV: literally, a mix of chronological and functional. This can be a good option if you want the benefits of a functional CV and the spotlight on your skills, competencies and experience, but without quite going all the way.

Example: Reverse chronological CV

FIONA DE GENERA

Curric House, Ulum Road, Huntingdon, G1Z JO8
Tel: 01234 567 890
Email: fidegenera@gmail.com

Profile

A chartered accountant and skilled finance director, I wish to capitalize on my technical knowledge and practical experience of financial accounting and taxation, in the role of ICAEW exam marker covering these modules: my starting point for a career in accountancy training.

Achievements

* Recognized in 2008 Who's Who of Britain's Business Elite as owner of one of Britain's most successful businesses.

Career History

2007–present   **Consultant, Wingover Logistics, Luton**

Wingover is a specialist international courier with an average annual turnover of £15 m.

---

* Advising on annual business strategy and assessing new investment opportunities to drive growth by 28 per cent year on year while maintaining profitability.
* Reviewing monthly management accounts and year end financial statements.
* Assisting with preparation of successful business tenders for international clients.

2005–2007　　　　　**Finance Director, Wingover Logistics**

* Responsible for devising and implementing financial strategy as a member of the Board.
* Working closely with the CEO and MD to shape overall business strategy and direction.
* Overseeing all financial operations and day-to-day accountancy, including preparing year end financial statements and draft tax computations.

2001–2005　　　　　**Manager Roles, Silva & Gold Chartered Accountants, Worksop**

Youngest ever manager after qualification for this national firm with £150 m annual fee income.

2003–2005　　　　　**Audit Department Manager**

* Promoted to be part of the eight-strong audit management team, with a staff of 30.
* Specializing in charity accounts and larger private companies.
* Overseeing accounts production and auditing using an analytical review approach.

2001–2003　　　　　**Small Business Unit Manager**

* Overseeing teams of 1–10 preparing accounts for small businesses, sole traders and partnerships.
* Co-ordinating and supervising a pool of 25 staff as part of a four-strong management team.
* Assistant training manager for students.

| 1998–2001 | **Audit Junior/Senior, Silva & Gold Chartered Accountants** |

Professional Memberships
  * Member of the Association of Chartered Accountants (2001)

Education

2001	Association of Chartered Accountants
1998	BA (Hons) 2:1 in Tourism and Leisure, University of Truro
1994	3 A Levels
1992	10 GCSEs

IT Skills
  * Sage Line 50 and Viztopia accounting software
  * Microsoft Office Suite

Further Details
  * Qualified First Aider (2006)
  * Full clean driving licence

To convert this to a functional CV is relatively straightforward:

Example: Functional CV

FIONA DE GENERA

Curric House, Ulum Road, Huntingdon, G1Z JO8
Tel: 01234 567 890
Email: fidegenera@gmail.com

Objective
A chartered accountant and successful finance director, I wish to capitalize on my technical knowledge of financial accounting and taxation in the role of ICAEW exam marker covering these modules. My intent is to pursue a career in accountancy training.

Key Skills and Competencies

Technical Knowledge
* Experience preparing, co-ordinating and auditing financial accounts using an analytical approach, for small, medium and large business clients and charities while at Silva & Gold.
* Overseeing management accounts, resolving complex financial planning and taxation issues, analyzing and making recommendations on new investments for the highly successful Wingover Logistics.

General Management
* Planning, allocating and managing resources as the Finance Director for Wingover Logistics: collaborating on four successful tenders, two for the highly competitive defence industry.
* Measuring and monitoring audit team activities to improve processes at Silva & Gold, saving 23 man hours per week across a team of 30 staff.

Leadership
* Successful organizational and strategic leadership as Finance Director of Wingover Logistics.
* Quickly promoted to lead the Small Business team at Silva & Gold, personally responsible for student training and staff development, before becoming Audit Manager within two years.

Achievements
* Recognized in 2008 Who's Who of Britain's Business Elite as owner of one of Britain's most successful businesses.
* Youngest ever manager at Silva & Gold upon qualification.

Professional Memberships
* Member of the Association of Chartered Accountants (2001)

IT Skills
* Sage Line 50 and Viztopia accounting software
* Microsoft Office Suite

Career Summary

2005–present	**Wingover Logistics, Heathrow**

Specialist international courier company: average annual turnover £15 m.

2007–present	**Consultant**
2005–2007	**Finance Director**
1998–2005	**Silva & Gold Chtd Accountants, Worksop**

National mid-tier independent accountancy firm: annual fee income £150 m.

2003–2005	**Audit Department Manager**
2001–2003	**Small Business Unit Manager**
1998–2001	**Audit Junior/Senior**

Education

2001	Association of Chartered Accountants
1998	BA (Hons) 2:1 in Tourism and Leisure, University of Truro

Further Details
* Qualified First Aider (2006)
* Full clean driving licence

Targeting a job and employer

Once you've got a handle on the industry or sector you're hoping to work in, and have structured your CV accordingly, you must tailor it to the specific role that you are after.

Responding to a job advert

This makes it easy: the job advert lays out a concise list of the key competencies and experience that a company is looking for in an ideal applicant. The priorities – whether a particular skill is essential or just nice to have – are usually made clear.

When assessing how well you meet the requirements of a job and what else you could offer, try comparing similar job adverts from other companies: ones for distant locations or other industries. There will be much overlap, but every now and again you may see a skill mentioned that you hadn't thought of; one you could sell as a benefit to this employer.

Automated scanning software

Each recruiter will be looking for evidence of skills in the CVs and covering letters they receive, and those processing a lot of applications may use automated scanning software to pick up these key words. For your CV to be as effective as possible, you need to achieve as many matches as you can. This doesn't mean simply repeating everything word for word. Recruiters want to see how well you meet the spec, not just that you can copy out their advert. Use your own phrasing, but include their key words.

Applying speculatively

The company you are targeting may have recruited into the role you'd like in the past, and with a bit of digging you can sometimes find old job adverts and descriptions online.

Other companies, whether in the same or different industry, may be recruiting into similar positions too. Check their job adverts as well, to establish the common competencies desired for all such roles.

So, how do you tailor your CV based on the details you've discovered about the role?

Profile

Include as many keywords and phrases from the job advert as you can, while making them specific and relevant to you. Promote transferable skills in lieu of experience if you are lacking experience, and give your rationale.

Employment History

Focus first on the demonstration of skill examples that show the essential skills required. Then add in the nice-to-have skills, before selling other benefits you can offer. Where possible draw your examples from similar roles or employment in a related industry that could benefit the position you are applying for.

Further skills

Again, relevance is the buzz word. You might want to show off all your skills, but not all of them are necessarily going to help you do *this* job better.

Interests

If one of your interests helps to demonstrate the skills required for the job, especially skills not shown at work, don't be afraid to describe the interest in a little more detail. Good team captains show leadership; club treasurers show financial acumen; part-time referees show judgement, decisiveness and in some cases conflict resolution; amateur dramatics suggests confidence and clear speaking in front of a large audience; a junior football coach might possess strong training and/or mentoring skills.

Functional CVs

Skills/Competencies

Your Skills or Competencies section should reflect in priority order the essential and nice-to-have skills as mentioned in the job advert, with supporting evidence. Add on any additional skills you could argue would be beneficial to the role, but leave out any that you really don't need to show.

All CVs

Achievements

Generally speaking, you want to have two or more bullet points before you create a separate achievements section, unless the achievement is particularly powerful, current and relevant to the role, in which case you could highlight just one.

Length

A targeted CV is likely to be shorter than the generic version. Given that not all examples will be relevant and, of those that are, you only want the best and most recent, your targeted Employment section should be significantly shorter than the one on your generic CV.

Relevance

Critical point: a fuller CV does not make you look any more proficient or experienced in the reader's eyes. All it says is that you waffle a lot or have not read the advert properly. Either way it's too much effort to dig through it for the information they want.

The employer

Research market, company and audience background as much as possible. Research can be very helpful for a number of reasons, but if you lack experience then some solid research can help you appear much more confident and knowledgeable, whilst ensuring you relate what experience you do have to the role.

Market

In some cases, especially larger corporations, you may not know which company is actually doing the hiring. This is because you are asked to send your CV to a recruitment agency. Obviously you won't be expected to know anything about the employer at first, but it can certainly help if you know a bit about the marketplace.

Company

Internet research can also give you insight into almost anything, including the:
* company culture
* kind of people they attract
* products they make
* main competitors for their business
* current and past performance.

Your reason for applying

If you don't already have a sound reason for wanting to work for a particular employer, then use your research to develop a rationale. It might seem a little strange to find a company first and then find a reason why you want to work for them, but it really is important. Otherwise you can imagine how the conversation might go:

Employer: 'So, how do I know that you really want to work for us?'
Applicant: 'Well, I applied for a job here didn't I?'
Employer: 'Hmm ... I mean why us, and not one of our competitors?'
Applicant: 'No one else is advertising at the moment.'
Employer: 'Thank you for your honesty. Next!'

When doing research, look out for any details that could help you explain not just 'why I'm looking for this kind of role' but 'why I really want this role in *your* company'. Having a positive story about why you'd love to work for a particular employer – it doesn't have to be long and involved – will shine through on your CV, and at interview.

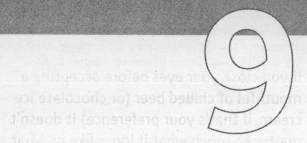

presenting
it perfectly

If you close your eyes before accepting a mouthful of chilled beer (or chocolate ice cream, if that's your preference) it doesn't matter so much what it looks like or what it's served in – the taste is what counts.

But a CV is a visual medium, so presentation is everything. That doesn't mean you can ignore content, but the layout and format of your CV will certainly set the reader's expectations.

* Which fonts, sizes and spacing should you use?
* How should you lay out points and sections clearly?
* What is the best way to make your CV easily readable?

Find answers to these questions here, and remember the importance of checking for any errors.

Different CV formats, and the pros and cons of each, are also touched on here to help you select the best for your circumstances. Is now the right time to be starring in a video CV?

Layout – how should a finished CV look?

The basic elements of good layout are drawn from years of scientific study into how people look at, read and process information. There are three things you must get right. A CV needs to be:

* legible
* scannable
* readable.

Making your CV legible

This simply means that someone can clearly make out the letters and words in your CV. It's amazing how often people get carried away making a page look 'pretty', or trying to fit too much onto two pages. Looking inviting is important, but don't forget the purpose of your CV is to be read and understood.

Here are some basic legibility guidelines:

Font

* **Don't** spend hours picking out complex fonts that look nice – these can be hard to read.
* **Do** use simple, clear fonts: for printed CVs, popular serif or sans serif fonts are both fine.

For online CVs, sans serif fonts are better as they are more legible on screen. If you are likely to send your CV on both paper and email, stay with sans serif.

Size

* **Don't t**hink tiny text will help you to cram in more words – they end up too small to read easily.
* **Don't** use text smaller than 10 point as it is too hard for most people to read easily.
* **Do** use a big enough text size. 11–12 point is normal for body text, 14–16 point for headings.

Line spacing

* **Don't** squash lines close together to fit in more text – closely-spaced lines are harder to follow.
* **Do** always leave single line spacing as your default and don't be tempted to decrease it, however much you are struggling to fit something in. If the text won't fit two pages, delete the least relevant point/s on your CV.

Font effects

* **Don't** overuse font effects, and particularly try to avoid *italics* and CAPITALS. Both are harder to read than standard text.
* **Do** use plain font as standard. Bold is acceptable for highlighting headings or specific points, but use it sparingly.

Text alignment

* **Don't** justify the text even if it looks 'tidier'. Justifying text makes the spacing between words uneven, and this makes it harder to read.
* **Do** always align text on the left-hand side, leaving the right side of the text 'ragged'.

Making your CV scannable (not the same as automated scanning!)

Once you have legible text, arranging it in a common sense, clear way is what makes it scannable: that is, easy for a person to scan through and quickly find what they want.

There are lots of things that make a CV more scannable:

* short text
* logical order
* clear headings and subheadings
* small chunks of information
* highlighted points: bullets, shading, dividing lines, boxed text
* use of white space.

Bear in mind that the more complex the formatting – things like shading, lines and boxes – the longer it will take you to edit and the more likely it is to end up looking different on someone else's screen. There is nothing wrong with a straightforward CV template in which the text is broken up with clear headings, bullet points and white space.

Some general guidelines

Don't:
* add extra, unnecessary detail
* change the order of your CV just to 'stand out from the crowd'
* make headings too small or remove subheadings to save space
* add extra text to make something look more important than it is
* run sentences into each other to save space
* fill every blank space on the page.

Do:
* keep text short
* make headings and subheadings clear
* have small chunks of information
* highlight key points.

Always:
* have plenty of white space
* have a logical order.

Making your CV readable

The final aim of your CV is to be readable – easy to read. Some of these points have already been covered while creating your generic CV, but it's worth checking again that your finished CV is still very readable.

What makes a CV readable (in addition to legibility and scannability, of course) is a mixture of word length and sentence length.

Word length

Longer words are harder for someone to read and understand quickly. The more long words you use, the less readable the text. It's not about 'dumbing down' – most people just prefer to read Plain English. Why use a long word when a short one will do?

Sentence length

Longer sentences are also harder to read and understand quickly. They tend to be more complex and may deal with more than one point or topic.

Do:
* aim for short sentences about single points or topics
* use short words
* put different or unrelated concepts in separate sentences.

Don't:
* overcomplicate things with overformal (long) sentences
* try to sound more business-like by using bigger words
* use too much jargon, especially long-worded jargon
* now add to sentences that you've already refined.

Always:
* read your CV out loud when checking readability. Do it more than once
* if you repeatedly stumble over any part, it's probably not very readable
* double-check to see whether you have used over-formal language or too much jargon
* try to use shorter words and sentences to say the same thing.

If you can pick up and read any part out loud without a hitch, it should be readable to most other people. However, don't leave it to chance – ask someone else to read it and see what they say.

Quality control

Quality control is usually the final stage of checks or tests before a finished product is sent out to customers. In the same way, this is the final step for your CV content. And that means **final**.

Don't get into quality control until you are sure there are no more changes to be made, otherwise you are just wasting your time.

When you think you are done, close your CV and take a break. If you have written your CV by hand up to this point, now is the time to get it typed. Then, with a clear mind, go back and proofread it to check for any errors.

Proofreading

It is notoriously hard to proofread your own work, even if you are an English professor. That's because you know what you wrote or rather, you know what you intended to write. Your brain tends to fill in any gaps and skim over errors without realizing.

Ideal is asking a friend with a good eye for detail – and great English – to proofread it for you. They could spot something you have overlooked again and again.

If you can't ask someone else to help, then read it out loud to yourself, very slowly. Pretend it's the first time you've ever seen it. Read every part aloud: even your own name, address, phone number, email address and all dates. This really helps show up any errors.

Computer spell checkers

Don't just rely on the computer's spell check to put everything right: it isn't able to understand the meaning of your words, and is therefore open to error.

During quality control if you find any mistakes that need correcting – a word, comma, space, bullet point, anything – then remember to do your quality control again afterwards.

It might seem like overkill but in the heat of last-minute changes, it's very easy to delete two words instead of one, ignore a missing phrase, mistype a date, misspell a name, or even add a random letter or symbol.

After all this hard work, your finished CV deserves to be completely error-free.

Format – factors to consider

Whenever you have a choice and the job advert doesn't specify, send a paper CV.

Advantages of a paper CV

* faster to read
* layout and text cannot be altered
* has a physical presence, is touchable
* can be read anywhere
* no compatibility issues

Disadvantages of a paper CV

* more expensive
* tempting to print bulk copies (instead of tailoring each one)
* can get damaged
* untraceable if lost: recruiter can't go back and print another copy
* post is slower than email – not ideal if you're applying at the last minute.

Paper considerations

* Good quality paper: ideally 120 gsm weight and slightly textured.
* Very pale coloured paper: pale cream, pale blue or pale grey, with black text.
* Print your covering letter on the same paper stock as your CV.
* Unless requested, use paperclips instead of staples.
* A4 envelope (remember to use a 'large' stamp) – brown or white irrelevant.

When sending a paper CV ensure pages are clearly numbered and also named; then, if the sheets do get separated, it's easy to see which ones belong together.

Digital CVs

The standard format for creating a digital CV is Microsoft Word. It is simple to use, easily editable and every employer should be able to open and read a .doc or .docx file. Beware of creating very complex layouts with too many boxes, outlines or embedded images: these can change format when viewed on other people's computers.

Another way to email your CV is as an Adobe PDF file. Adobe Acrobat Reader software is free online and enables you to open a PDF. The great advantage of PDFs is their layout and appearance is fixed and can't change, no matter what computer they are viewed on.

Before emailing your CV, check the filename is appropriate and begins with your own name: e.g. GeorgeClooneyCV.docx. When recruiters receive 500 CV files, almost all entitled 'CV.docx', working through them becomes extremely awkward. They'll thank you for making things easy.

Advantages of a digital CV

* zero printing, stationery and postage costs
* quick to arrive: great for last-minute applications
* pages can't be lost
* simple to post on internet job sites
* can easily be shared with other interested recruiters
* return receipts can let you know when/if it's been read
* automated scanning for keywords is simple.

Disadvantages of a digital CV

* can be shared/sent on without you knowing
* private details less likely to remain confidential
* file may get corrupted and be impossible to open

* file may not be compatible with other computers
* layout format may change when viewed on a different computer
* can only be read on a screen
* no physical qualities exist to help it stand out from other files.

Non-standard CV formats

This includes formats such as Video or Podcast CVs. Yes, there are more ways than 2D to get your message and selling points across. No, you don't have to (and shouldn't) try to be different just for the sake of it.

Alternative CV formats such as Video CVs are particularly appropriate for some industries, especially those focused on visual aspects such as entertainment, advertising, marketing, media, technology and design. While there is also an increasing number of people from more traditional business backgrounds exploring the video CV format, many employers may not have seen one before and would not expect to receive one. This could count for or against you.

Generally speaking, the advice is to use a CV format that will:
* be accepted by the employer, and
* give you the biggest advantage.

CVs for overseas applications

Whoever the employer and wherever they are based, it never hurts to:
* choose one language (English or local) and stick to it throughout your CV
* place the most relevant parts at the beginning
* keep it brief and aim for a maximum of two pages.

10

complementing your CV

Your CV will only get read if your covering letter is sufficiently enticing, so in a way this chapter is the beginning. Its position at the end of this book makes sense though: you should only start a covering letter once you've finished your targeted CV.

A covering letter is a teaser, to encourage the recipient to read your CV. It should contain six things – the briefer the better – and reflect key words and phrases from your CV without repeating large chunks.

Covering letters are quicker to write than CVs, but are still worth taking time to perfect. This is your letter of introduction, without which all the time spent on your CV could be wasted.

Most of the hard work is now done. If you look after your generic CV and keep Chapters 8–10 handy, you should be in a good position for your next move – whatever it is.

Covering letters

It's rare that a recruiter opens an envelope to find nothing but a CV inside. As a rule, a CV is always sent with a one-page covering letter or email that:

* names the role you are applying for
* highlights why you would be perfect for this role at this company
* encourages the recipient to read your CV and invite you for interview.

It's fair to say that this letter is, in many ways, even more important than your CV. A good letter guarantees that someone will at least skim through your CV. Dull, irrelevant or badly-written letters beg to go straight in the bin – swiftly followed by your CV, however good it was.

Your covering letter needs to seduce the reader. It should take them by the hand, pat the seat and say: 'Come and sit down. I've got an amazing CV for you to read. Look – this person has everything you could possibly want, all you need to do is see that for yourself.' Once they start to read, they'll be hooked.

Letters that do the literary equivalent of shrugging their shoulders and saying: 'Here, have a quick peek at this CV. It's quite good, you might even like some of it,' are not doing as much as they should to help you. Worse still, if they mutter: 'It's a lot to ask but I'm hoping something in this CV might just catch your eye if you have the patience to give it a proper read', then all your time spent learning to write an amazing CV has been wasted.

What type of covering letter should you use?

Many people feel that you should have a different type of covering letter for each type of application. Job adverts in the press vs. online job adverts, employer vs. recruitment agency adverts, responsive vs. speculative letters, for example. However, with the possible exception of purely speculative applications, every covering letter or email basically needs to say the same things. It's how you say them that matters.

What to include in a covering letter

You can include up to six points, ideally all fitting on one side of paper. Have a separate short paragraph for each.

1 Say clearly why you are sending your CV

Are you:

* answering an advert?
* writing speculatively, to ask if there are any opportunities for someone with your skills?
* sending a CV because a mutual contact suggested you do so?

2 Very briefly, say why you are an ideal person for this/a job

* What skills and experience do you have that would be useful to them?
* What would help you do this job better than others might be able to?
* Direct them to your enclosed/attached CV to see proof of this, and more.

3 State why you would like to work for this particular company

It might be due to:

* reputation
* culture
* performance
* feedback from acquaintances who work there
* personal interest in/passion for their products
* location
* opportunities for progression
* concern for the environment
* any other sensible reason you can think of.

4 Add any other important details that aren't already in your CV

You may wish to:

* explain that you are about to relocate or are willing to do so if needed
* give details of your current salary – only if specifically asked for
* confirm that you have a valid driving licence
* mention a relevant training course or qualification that you are due to start very soon
* be creative and add a testimonial from one of your appraisals or references.

5 Say what response you would like from the recipient

This might be:

* an interview for the job advertised (do mention if you are unavailable, for example, away on holiday)
* an initial conversation with someone about potential opportunities
* written details of current vacancies
* your CV to be kept on file
* your CV to be forwarded/recommended for consideration, if sent to a personal contact
* anything else you would like them to do.

6 End your letter with any action you intend to take (if you do intend to)

Let them know that you:

* are going to telephone next week to check your application has arrived safely
* will wait to hear back from them
* welcome the chance to discuss further at interview
* look forward to meeting them.

Covering emails

Ideally a covering email can be read on one screen without having to scroll down. In most respects it should be exactly the same as the equivalent covering letter:

* Use the same language, layout and content as a printed letter, although you can delete postal address details and dates as this is tagged automatically.
* Put the vacancy you are applying for in the subject line of the email to make it easy for the recipient, especially if it's a recruitment agency handling lots of vacancies.

Targeting your covering letter

Your starting point for a targeted CV is your generic CV, which you edit according to a specific opportunity – ideally based on the job advert if there is one.

Your starting point for a targeted covering letter is your targeted CV. There should be no such thing as a generic covering letter.

Application forms

Application forms are often asked for because CVs can vary dramatically in style and content. As a CV writer, you are entitled to highlight whichever points you want – and to play down any parts you don't feel proud of. This can make CVs quite hard to compare. An application form can be much more specific, ensuring everyone submits similar information and often asking questions way beyond the remit of any CV. Check that both documents you send are consistent. It doesn't look good if, for example, the dates of your qualifications on your CV and application form don't agree – especially when you are claiming that attention to detail is one of your strengths.

Congratulations!

The hard work is over, but before you lick that stamp or click that mouse, check you have a copy of everything so that you remember it when you're invited to interview.

Keep your generic CV fresh by feeding it updated material regularly. When the perfect opportunity appears, you'll have more time to spend doing the refining, research and targeting that makes a CV truly irresistible.